A
small
child's
glimpse
into
Eternity

There Is A God In
Heaven That Revealeth
Secrets

(Daniel 2:28)

Heaven Revealed

A five-year-old drowning victim tells of her out-of-body visitation in Heaven.

The Miracle of Melody Meade
Told by her parents,
Larry and Dollie Meade

I thank You, O Father, Lord of heaven and earth,
because You have hidden these things from the
wise and prudent, and have revealed them unto
babes" (Matthew 11:25).

CONTENTS

Acknowledgements:

There have been many who have helped in getting this story ready for publication.

We give a special thanks to Curtis Grant who without the writing help he gave we would have never gotten the story written.

Thank you to the following individuals for their counsel, guidance, advice, and proof reading that made this book possible: Frank Neville, Naomi Whitehouse, Marybeth Bowles, Linda Bullock, Prof. Willy Dharmaraj, Dorothy Basham, and Lana Henderson.

"For now we see through a glass, darkly; but then face-to-face: now I know in part; but then shall I know even as also I am known" (1 Corinthians 13:12)

Dedication

Dedicated to those who rallied to help, when a little girl's lifeless body was floating in a backyard swimming pool. Melody asks that we dedicate her story to "Papaw" (Pastor Nolan Sluder, her "adopted" grandfather) who continued to give her mouth-to-mouth resuscitation, as others kept on praying.

We also dedicate this book to the memory of the many friends who had encouraged us to get this story into print, but have since passed beyond the vale into the eternal reality that we now attempt to tell about. We especially mention the late Pastor Carey Puckett and his wife Rose who had looked forward to this book. We also wish to honor the memory of Melody's paternal grandmother Velma Meade, and we remember Millie Sluder who became Melody's "adopted"grandmother.

Likewise, we lovingly dedicate these pages to each reader who, together with us, desires to look, even through this "glass, darkly" into the joys of Heaven.

— Larry, Dollie, and Melody

Endorsements

You made a good choice when you decided to read this book. I have been preaching the Gospel for over seventy-two years and have over sixty-six years of uninterrupted ordination in the Assemblies of God. Melody considers me to be her grandfather and to me that is a great honor. Larry and Dollie Meade have been a part of our extended family since 1966.

Several books have been written about death or near death experiences. Please allow me to speak to the accuracy and authenticity of HEAVEN REVEALED. Much time, prayer and thought was spent before Melody and her parents decided to share this miraculous event with the reading public. After the decision to share Melody's trip to Heaven with others, great care was given to tell the experience exactly as it happened. This miracle happened in our back yard at 13831 County Road, Tyler, Texas. I was there and experienced it with them. It is my opinion that Melody, Larry and Dollie Meade have told it as it truly happened!

Nolan Sluder, Pastor
Author: *Let the Ages Roll, Journey West, How to Fix Your Social Security Through Real Estate Investing*

I heard this story in part for the first time nearly 30 years ago, yet it is as fresh today as the first time I ever heard it. It does not need to be embellished or exaggerated, it is as innocent as the heart of a child. The power of truth is in the telling of it. This is that kind of story and it is indeed powerful. Years ago, I read a poem about a man looking for a party. He was disappointed in his quest. He thought out loud, surely there must be an unending party somewhere on earth. His love for a party was a driving addiction and just when he was about to give up his search, he saw snatches of light and heard music breaking through from another world. It was a place as real as the one where he was living. It was a prepared place for a prepared people, it was heaven. In this story you will be able to see, through the eyes of Melody as a child, snatches of light and hear the music of this wonderful place.

Cleddie Keith,
Senior Pastor-Revivalist
Heritage Fellowship, Florence, KY
Author: *Praying the Lord's Prayer*

The first time I met Melody Meade she was just a few days old when her parents brought her to my wedding. She has been like a member of my own family and her parents have been lifelong friends.

As a toddler she experienced a visitation to heaven. Not only did it have a profound impact on her, but also to everyone who heard the story. My spirit still soars when I think of her heavenly experience. For years people have urged her father and missionary evangelist Larry Meade to write this book.

We are grateful to Melody, her mother and father, Larry and Dollie Meade, for the impact they have made to thousands around the world with this miraculous story.

Dr. Bob Rodgers,
Sr. Pastor, Evangel World Prayer Center
Louisville, KY USA
Author: *The 21 Day Fast,*
      101 Reasons to Fast

I have known Larry and Dollie Meade since the early 80's when we were both serving as pastors of small congregations in Western Kentucky. They have been a guest in my church pulpit and have always preached with God's blessing and anointing.

It was an honor for me to interview them a few years ago on our Daystar station's Celebration in the Tri State area around Huntington, WV. I have heard the story of Melody's accident many times, but I am still moved to the brink of emotion every time it is told. Because Larry, Dollie, and Melody have traveled as evangelists as well as missionaries to different regions of the world, this story has been told to countless thousands, and it never gets old! Now is your opportunity to hear the firsthand account of a little girls' return from a death experience.

Dr. Richard Clifton
Pastor, General Manager, Daystar TV
Channel WTSF-61, DT44, Ashland, KY

Yes, Heaven Is Real!

Only God can reveal what is real.

Foreword
BY MELODY'S PARENTS
Larry & Dollie Meade

All primitive societies have had some type of belief in an after-life, where each person goes when the heart stops beating, the lungs stop breathing, and the body ceases to function. When what we call death comes, what is next? The American Indian believes he goes to the *Happy Hunting Ground*, while the Hindu desires to become one with Brahma, to get off the life-cycle and not be reincarnated.

In John 14:2, Jesus said, *"I go to prepare a place for you."* What is that place? When do we go there? What about angels? Will we see them and have any connection to them? Will there be children in Heaven? Are there really mansions there? What could they be possibly constructed from?

Will we know one another in Heaven? Will we recognize and know someone with whom we were not personally acquainted with while living on earth? Can God send a message from a person in Heaven to someone on earth?

How will we communicate? Are there thorns on the roses? What about the streets of gold, or the water? Will we eat there? If so, what about the food? Will it be of necessity that we eat, or will it simply be to enjoy the pleasing taste of Heaven's food?

No doubt, we could think of hundreds of questions to ask about Heaven, and many of them will never be answered until we finally arrive.

In this book, you will have some insights into the future home called Heaven, supported by God's holy scriptures, as we compared them against the out-of-body visitation in Heaven that our five-year-old daughter experienced, and then related to us.

We have shared this story over the years in sermons, through interviews on radio and television, and in personal conversations, which have been a source of comfort and encouragement to many people.

Here, we tell you how our daughter drowned in a backyard swimming pool, and later told us how she departed from her lifeless body, and went to Heaven.

You will read about what she saw and heard there. She had just turned five years old a few weeks prior to this experience, so she did not have the Biblical knowledge to create a story that would be verified by so many different scriptures. She simply was relating what she experienced.

Please understand that these things, which she had seen and told, are from the perspective of a small child. Sometimes she did not know how to actually verbalize what she was trying to describe so we will describe what the Bible tells us about Heaven. Likewise, this is how we share it with you. There are some research facts that did not flow into the topical chapter headings, and these are included in the *Addendum* at the back.

Toward the end especially, you will see how such a small child could not have fathomed the depth of this revelation. God gave us the interpretation so it could first minister to us, and then could minister to others.

Now, let us begin the story of Melody's journey to Heaven, as I begin to tell how it has affected us personally...

"It was Dollie's anguished voice, as she kept shouting out, crying for help."

Mayday!
Mayday!
Mayday!

I will never forget an extremely hot day in May, down in Tyler, Texas. I had taken my wife Dollie and our five-year-old daughter, Melody, to the home of Pastor Nolan and Millie Sluder. My brother, Dennis, was there as well. The four of us were having a business conversation, and were deeply engrossed in discussing the details.

We had been standing in the Sluder's front yard discussing the problem. Pastor Sluder and I decided to go into the house and make a phone call. My hand was in mid-air from hanging up the phone when I heard a blood-curdling scream from outside the house. It was Dollie's anguished voice shouting out and crying for help. I leaped from my chair and looked through the window. There at the swimming pool, I saw why she was so terrified. Lying face down, floating in the center of the pool, was our precious daughter.

I knew that Melody had not yet learned to swim, and that part of the pool was deep, far over her head. It was the most heart-wrenching feeling of desperation I had ever felt in my life. It looked like our only child had drowned in the backyard swimming pool.

When the sea overpowers a ship, the distress call is *Mayday! Mayday!*

On that dreadful day in May, a priceless treasure, far more valuable than a ship, was down in the water. Our hearts and hopes were sinking too. The distress was so great. Our signals seemed so weak.

But let us never forget the range of God's great receiver! Whatever the stress, or whatever the distress, He says, *"Call unto me, and I will answer you, and shew you great and mighty things, which you do not know"* (Jeremiah 33:3).

Above the raging of our personal storm, God picked up our signal. He not only changed things on earth, but in the days that followed, He began to show some profound things about Heaven through the eyes of a little child.

"For five to six months,
until the mother gave birth, this
special child was also growing
inside our hearts."

Heaven Revealed

Her Name Shall Be...

We were so sure of the name that Dollie began to buy baby clothes for a baby girl.

Before I continue, let me go back in time and share why Melody was such a special child to us. Dollie and I had been married for more than fourteen years, and we still had no children.

Dollie had a difficult time as the years passed, especially at church on Mother's Day. They would honor all the mothers, but she was unable to take part. It was a happy day for others, but it was a sad time for her. We had no child.

Against this dark backdrop, we had a beautiful turnaround. A missionary friend called, asking if we wanted to adopt a baby. A pastor whom he knew was searching for a couple in the ministry who would like to choose a child of their own. There was a young lady in this church who was pregnant, and unmarried. The company she worked for was on strike and she had returned to her hometown to visit her family during this time. She began going to this pastor's church and had received Christ as her personal Savior.

The young father of the child came and talked to the pastor about marriage, but he had no interest in God or the church. This new convert and mother-to-be refused to marry him under those conditions. This is when our friend called us.

We happily and readily accepted this offer to adopt, and we agreed to receive the baby as soon as it was born. Whether it was a boy or girl, this was left in God's hands. We also agreed to pay all medical expenses for the young lady.

For five to six months, until the mother gave birth, this special child was also growing inside our hearts. During this time, we were ministering in India. One day we were looking through a book of names and their meanings. We wanted to pick a name for both a boy and a girl, and learn what these names meant. Nothing we found had that certain click or connection that seemed just right.

One afternoon, as I was praying and preparing for an evening service, suddenly a name dropped into my spirit. I was not particularly thinking or praying about a name, but *Melody Ann* came to mind. I was so positive that God had just given me our baby's name that we never looked for another. We were convinced the baby would be a girl, and her name would be *Melody Ann*. Melody means *"song"* and Ann means, according to the book we read, *"full of grace, mercy and prayer; or favored grace."* Melody has Greek origins; Ann has Hebrew origins. *The name of this special child that God is giving to us is found in the two original languages of the Bible!*

Actually, in our hearts, we had both wanted a girl. Now, we fully believed that God had just confirmed He was answering our heart's desire. So, what did Dollie do? She went out into the stores of India and began to buy pink clothes for our coming baby girl! The Indians were somewhat puzzled by this, as they most always want a boy for their first child.

It did not seem puzzling to Dollie. God had given us a girl's name. She was just coordinating the colors!

Heaven Revealed

God Gives Us
Our Baby Girl

A Special Mother's Day

We were due to return home from India in early May. We arrived at the JFK Airport in New York and phoned my sister, Mary Jean, who lived in the Washington D.C. area. We had intended to go through there to pick up our car. We were elated when she told us, "Your pastor, Carey Puckett, called. He said, 'They are trying to get in touch with you. The baby has been born, and it's a girl!'" Joy and happiness filled our hearts, because God had confirmed our faith.

My brother-in-law, Ross Carey, later asked Dollie, "How did it feel to become a mother in a phone booth at the New York airport?" She exclaimed, "It felt wonderful!"

While still at the JFK Airport, we immediately booked another flight for Dollie. She headed for the town where the baby was born, to receive our special delivery girl!

After I had gotten our car, I drove to Mayfield, Kentucky, arriving in Mayfield the next afternoon just in time to go to the home of our pastors, Carey and Rose Puckett. Right away, Rose and I were in her car, to begin a three-hour drive to Memphis, to meet Dollie and Melody Ann at the airport.

Dollie came walking down the ramp, smiling from ear to ear. She gently placed this brand new, three-day-old bundle of joy into my arms. At that point, I was so excited, lost for words. Maybe I stammered out something like, *"It's a father! I'm a seven-pound girl!"* She was the most beautiful baby girl in the whole world!

People on the plane had asked Dollie how old her baby was, and when she replied, "she is three days old," they were surprised she was out of hospital and on an airplane with a newborn baby! Dollie just smiled at them.

The next Sunday was Mother's Day. Unlike other years when Dollie was so sad, now it was a time of great personal joy. It was like Hannah's words from Dollie's mouth: *"For this child I prayed; and the LORD granted my petition which I asked of him: Therefore also I have lent (her) to the Lord"* (I Samuel 1:27, 28).

We took our very own, nine-day-old baby to be dedicated as our loan to the Lord on this Special Mother's Day.

We believe that before she was born, God had ordained for Melody to be ours. We are confident she was His gift to us. You will see later how this thought is so significant. This was our life buoy when she was down in the water, and we were sinking so low, and we made our distress cry to Him.

In the Bible, you read many times where a child was not raised by the birth parents, and yet God had a special plan and purpose for that life. Moses, though he was nursed by his mother, was raised as the son of Pharaoh's daughter. Samuel, as a young child, was brought to the house of the Lord in Shiloh to be raised and trained by Eli. Esther was an orphan in a strange country, and God exalted her to greatness. Each of these three individuals had a unique purpose in His will.

Just suppose this young mother that I told you about had chosen the option of abortion. It had become legal just a few years before Melody was born. Think of all the lives that have been lost since 1973 when the Supreme Court made its decision to legalize abortion.

Since that decision, it is estimated that over 53 million babies have been aborted in America up to now! That is more than the combined populations of Canada and Australia!

Think about it: *Hitler killed over 6 million people in the Jewish holocaust, and historians abhor such horrific injustice. YET the number of lives lost by abortion since 1973 already eclipses the holocaust by 46 million! And still, there are people who persist to say that the Supreme Court Justices were right to uphold abortion.*

An entire generation has been lost through legalizing the termination of a baby's life. We have lost leaders in every field, and the prosperity of our nation has been greatly diminished because of this tragic disregard for a person's human right to exist and to fulfill his or her purpose on earth.

God said to Jeremiah: *"Before I formed you in the belly I knew you; and before you came forth out of the womb I set you apart, and I ordained you as a prophet to the nations"* (Jeremiah 1:5).

Over the years, Dollie and I have placed great

value on various ministries and agencies that encourage people to choose adoption instead of abortion. Every believer should support them in prayer and should ask God to give them creative ways to spread their message.

To families whose lives have been traumatized by the scars of abortion, or to some member of the family who is considering abortion, we can say with confidence that God guides you from where you are. In Christ, there is freedom from the guilt of the past, and there is hope in your choice for the future. Through His wisdom and strength, choose life.

"I remember trying to get back to the steps. I could see them under water but was too far away. I was also too far from the edge of the pool to grab it either. I tried many times to push myself above the water and scream for help but every time I came up I just took in more water. I tried 5-6 times then everything went black...."

— Melody Meade

"What a wonderful sound,
to hear our sweet baby cry!
Our hearts rejoiced with
new hope!"

Heaven Revealed

"Lord, Give Our Baby Back Again!"

Now, let me return to Melody's story, and back to the tragic event where we found her floating facedown in the swimming pool.

While we were in conversation in front of Pastor Sluder's home, Melody had come near, trying to tell us something. She had been playing at the pool with the Sluder's oldest daughter, Pat, who was ready to leave. Pat fastened her float to the buoy rope. Then the rope was hooked to the side of the pool.

Melody had taken the buoy rope that was no longer in use, and she tied it around her own little plastic ring. She came to ask her mom and dad to come and see how she had taught herself to "swim."

To this five-year-old girl, it was something

she had accomplished on her own, and she wanted us to see it. But we were too busy and we ignored her. She went back to the pool.

When she returned, the rope had come loose and had floated out to the deep end of the pool, taking the ring with it. She decided to walk out and get it; not knowing the water was deep. She stepped off into the water that was over her head.

Years later, Melody still recalls this frantic scene from her childhood: *"I remember trying to get back to the steps. I could see them under water but was too far away. I was also too far from the edge of the pool to grab it either. I tried many times to push myself above the water and scream for help but every time I came up I just took in more water. I tried 5-6 times then everything went black..."*

I heard Dollie's chilling scream, looked out the window, and saw Melody's body floating in the pool. You can only imagine the crushing of my heart and the sense of horror in this daddy's mind.

I raced toward the pool as fast as I could run. When I reached the pool, Dollie had already jumped in to get Melody, and she was bringing her out when I arrived. I knelt down and took her little limp body from Dollie's arms.

Those of us who were there were not medical professionals, but none of us detected any sign of life. We could not find a pulse or heartbeat. Her lips and mouth were blue, and she was completely lifeless.

So many thoughts race through the mind at such a time as this: *"How long had she been in the pool? What will life be like without our only child?"*

Pastor Nolan Sluder remembers: "Larry was holding her body, saying "Oh God, don't let our baby die!" Actually, I was in such a state of shock and despair, I don't remember what I was saying.

Then Pastor Sluder stepped up and took Melody from my arms, and he laid her down near the pool. He began to give her mouth-to-mouth resuscitation. He says, "I gave her about seven or eight breaths before anything happened. Then, one eye flickered a little bit." He gave her three or four more breaths and turned her head to the side.

I was kneeling there beside Melody's body, just saying, *"Jesus! Jesus! Jesus!"* I didn't know anything else to do but call on the Jesus who said, *"I am the resurrection and the Life"* (John 11:25) and we really needed the Power of His resurrection Life!.

During all of this, I heard Dollie pray, **"Lord, you gave her to us once; now give her back to us again!"**

We estimated later it must have been two or three minutes before anything happened. But, as Dollie uttered these words, something began to change. Melody's eye flickered. A red-pop liquid that she had drunk earlier in the day, along with water, began to come out of her mouth and she began to cry. What a wonderful sound, to hear our sweet baby cry!

Sister Sluder had called the emergency room and they said to wrap Melody in a blanket and bring her to the hospital as fast as possible. Because the hospital was several miles away, Pastor Sluder drove at break-neck speed, with his lights and flashers on.

I was holding Melody in the passenger seat, and she screamed and cried all the way to the hospital. When we arrived they took her directly into the emergency room and began to give her oxygen.

We were anxiously waiting in the emergency

room where they had taken Melody. What was going to happen now? Will she be alright?

After some time we heard her screaming and crying. I listened for what seemed like forever. Suddenly, overcome with concern for our daughter, I headed back to the room where she was being attended to. Dollie had heard the receptionist call back to the room and say "The father is coming."

When I walked in, they tried to cover the blood on the sheet, which had also dripped to the floor. Rather emotionally, I said, "Where is the Doctor? The nurses were trying to get needles into the veins of her arms to check the oxygen level in her blood. I demanded the presence of a doctor proclaiming, "She has been traumatized enough." The doctor came and they finally checked the oxygen in her blood.

She was scared, and wanted her daddy! But instead, they gave her a balloon and were reading to her hoping to calm her while trying to insert a needle. She screamed and cried all the more.

Approximately one hour from the time we pulled her out of the pool and after having been on oxygen 20-30 minutes, they said, the oxygen level of the blood was only about half of the normal amount she should have had, so they decided to keep her in the hospital overnight. They wanted to keep monitoring her to make sure there was no brain damage due to the lack of oxygen.

The next day, all medical tests proved Melody was back to normal! God had given her to us the first time, and He had now given her to us again!

The doctor said that we had received a miracle, and the nurses often came from their workstation into her room to see this "Miracle Child" that had no brain damage.

The next day after coming home from the hospital, I was cleaning the pool in which she had drown. She came out and sat down on the top step leading into the pool. I did not want to make her afraid of the water but did not want to force her in it either. I casually told her she could get in the water if she wanted to. She asked if it would hurt to get her shorts wet. I told it would be ok. She got down in the water and I asked her if she remembered what happened.

She took her hand and went up and down in the water three times and said "Glub! Glub! Glub! I tried to call for help but no one heard me."

The glory and wonder of her experience had taken away all fear of the water and she learned to swim that summer. Thanks be to God for His great mercy to us.

Melody
begins to tell
how she went
to Heaven...
and we begin
to check out
her story.

"The angel that brought me set
me down on a gold street at a
big pearl gate."

Heaven Revealed

Heavenly Escort

An angel takes Melody to the Gate.

After leaving the hospital, Melody began to tell how she had gone to Heaven and what happened to her while we adults were trying to revive her lifeless body. For many days she would speak about her visitation in Heaven, and then would stop talking about it. Later, she would recount another memory, which would lead us to ask her many questions.

Melody had never been a child to fantasize and to make up stories. We had taught her to be truthful. She loved Jesus dearly, and we had confidence in her truthfulness. But we listened intently to each part of her story, to verify it with the details in scripture.

We wanted to make sure these things were not the imagination of a child.

If any part of her account did not agree with what God says in the Bible, we could not accept it or share it.

We knew that even the apostle Paul checked out his own personal revelation (Galatians 1:15-2:6). How much more would God expect us to confirm this incredible tale from our own daughter.

We discovered that many things Melody told us about Heaven were clearly confirmed in the Bible. Other things were not specifically stated in the scriptures, but appeared to be very possible or likely by similar events revealed in the Word.

As she had stepped into the deep water over her head, Melody struggled up and down in the water. She said, "I tried to call for help, but no one heard me." As she was sinking into the water of the pool, it is evident by Scripture that her spirit left her body. Then, she begins to tell what happened:

"An angel came and took me by the hand, and we began to fly through a wide open black sky. There was no light or stars, but I was not scared. The angel that brought me set me down on a gold street at a gate, which was an entrance into some place. The angel seemed to be the size of a normal person."

In another part of her story, Melody said

that she had seen large, towering angels. But here, she says the angel was "the size of a normal person." As we prepared to explain this *discrepancy* in our daughter's story, we adults certainly learned a lot about angels.

Remember, this is a small child speaking. She cannot yet read even basic Bible stories. She has never studied angelology, *but yet this five-year-old girl is telling us about Heaven and things that you read in systematic theology books.* This is not a theory that a child wants to know about. She has just experienced Heaven, and we adults are asking the questions! It's amazing what we confirmed from scriptures, even about angels.

In the Bible, God's angels exercise no power of their own; they minister by His power. Because angels move under God's delegated authority, His authority and power work through them. The apostle Jude gave this as a pattern for believers to resist the enemy. The Book of Jude says that even Michael, the archangel, submitted himself to God and then said to the devil, *"The Lord rebuke you"* (v. 9).

Because Michael was submitted, he had God's *delegated authority*, and the devil feared *the same authority that had cast him from Heaven* (Luke 10:18; Isaiah 14:12-15).

Secular history records the night of a terrible *death plague* when the armies of Sennacherib, king of Assyria, came against God's people. The Bible says this *'plague'* was by just one angel, with delegated authority:

"Then the angel of the Lord went forth, and smote in the camp of the Assyrians a hundred and fourscore and five thousand: and when they arose early in the morning, behold, they were all dead corpses" (Isaiah 37:36).

At the end, God will deal with Satan by the delegated authority of just one angel:

"And I saw an angel come down from heaven, having the key of the bottomless pit and a great chain in his hand. And he laid hold on the dragon, that old serpent, which is the Devil, and Satan, and bound him a thousand years, And cast him into the bottomless pit, and shut him up..." (Revelation 20:1-3).

So, without hesitation, I affirm my belief that one angel, no larger than a normal person, took Melody by the hand, and took her from Tyler, Texas, to the great heavenly land in a moment of time.

In the Bible, a poor man named Lazarus was *"carried by the angels into Abraham's bosom"* (Luke 16:22). This is a Bible example of a person at death being received by God and transported into the new realm of life. I believe this happened to Melody as an angel escorted her to the entrance of Heaven.

Angels are an innumerable host of ministering spirits that do the work of God (Hebrews 1:14; 12:22). Jesus said that He could have called *"twelve legions of angels,"* to be sent from Heaven to help Him (Matthew 26:53). One day, He *"called a little child unto Him,"* and then He said, *"Take heed that you despise not one of these little ones; for I say unto you, that in heaven their angels do always behold the face of my Father which is in heaven"* (Matthew 18:2-10).

He speaks of *"little ones"* such as our small, drowning daughter who was facedown in the swimming pool. Christ says *"their angels"* are sent forth to help them. In other words, God's angels are "*their* angels" (possessive case). He assigns *specific* angels to *specific* people. I believe that Melody's *spirit*, her *inside-person*, departed from that little five-year-old body in the swimming pool, and was taken by her angel into Heaven.

Checking out Melody's story, Dollie asked her, "How long were you in Heaven?" She replied, *"ten minutes."*

Sometime later, Dollie asked her again, "How long were you in Heaven?" She was unshaken, as she answered firmly, "I already told you, *ten minutes*." I believe that she was transported beyond the realm of earthly time, where it was only a few minutes back here on earth. She was ushered by an angel into the eternal realm, where she had a visitation that takes many earth-hours for her to tell about.

The Bible says, *"one day is with the Lord as a thousand years, and a thousand years as one day"* (2 Peter 3:8).

When asked to describe the angels that she saw, Melody said that some angels' wings appeared to be short and others appeared to be long. She said the material of angels' wings or clothes are soft like velvet, but not exactly like our velvet. At first, she could not describe exactly, in earth terms, what angel wings were like. Then, she added, "They were like *feathers*," a small child's description of wings so simple that we wondered why anyone would think otherwise!

As we think upon angels and how they relate to children, the scene of a famous painting comes to mind. It depicts two small children on a deteriorating bridge that spans a dangerous ravine. Hovering over the two children is a strong angel. That painting shows what a mother can expect when she submits to the scriptures, bringing up her children under *delegated authority*. The Bible says: *"For this cause ought the woman to have a sign of authority on her head, because of the angels"* (1 Corinthians 11:10) (ASV).

In the custom of that day, it was a sign, something like a wedding band, that said,

"I am under delegated authority, as are God's angels that cover my children."

Heaven Revealed

On A "Gold Street" Looking Down

At the Gate. A Glimpse back to earth.

Melody's spirit had just departed from her body in a backyard swimming pool. An angel the size of a normal person took her by the hand and flew with her toward Heaven. In an interview, she told about a glimpse back to earth, as she was entering the gate.

"After a short trip through dark space, the angel set me down on this 'gold street.' I looked down through it and could see the swimming pool, along with my parents and grandparents trying to revive me."

After this, Melody saw other angels, gigantic angels. Before we check them with the Bible, what about the *"gold street"* that this little girl saw? And what can we learn from her glimpse back to earth and what she saw back upon the earth? We can only define what she saw by what

God's Word reveals.

Perhaps you have heard a person say, "Heaven's streets are *paved* with gold." Actually, the Bible says they are *pure gold*.

Melody said there was a street of gold, but it was different and finally after not knowing how to describe it, said "it was gold but you could see through it."

John saw the New Jerusalem, and said... *"the street of the city was pure gold, as it were transparent glass"* (Revelation 21:21).

Now, you read Melody's testimony, how she *"saw right through"* the *"gold street,"* and she saw those down on earth trying to revive her lifeless body. And you might say, "Of course, she did! That's how Heaven is designed. It has a pure-gold, transparent street! All Bible scholars know that!"

This little five-year-old girl didn't know that -- until she had this out-of-body experience, and it was revealed to her. And some church-going adults wouldn't know it, until they see it in Scripture.

It is impossible for the finite mind to understand God's infinite designs.

That is why the scriptures say:

"Eye has not seen, nor ear heard, Nor has it entered into the heart of man the things, which God has prepared for those who love Him. But God has revealed them to us through His Spirit" (1 Corinthians 2:9-10).

I really can't explain how God designed it. But it makes me want to take Melody by the hand, and with child-like faith say, "I believe that your grandmothers and others are looking down upon us through the transparent bottom of Heaven!"

Isn't that what the Book of Hebrews says?

"Wherefore seeing we also are compassed about with so great a cloud of witnesses, let us lay aside every weight, and the sin which so easily besets us, and let us run with patience the race that is set before us..." (Revelation 12:1).

In Melody's story, the angel brought her to a gate that led into Heaven. We don't know which gate it was, for Heaven has many gates. In what we could call the *"Celestial City,"* the *New Jerusalem* alone has twelve gates.

In the Spirit, the apostle John said that this beautiful City...

"had a wall great and high, and had on the east three gates; on the north three gates; on the south three gates; and on the west three gates" (Revelation 21:12-13).

Each of the twelve gates is one solid pearl...

"And the twelve gates were twelve pearls; every individual gate was of one pearl" (Revelation 21:21).

Centuries before this, the prophet had expressed the desire of God's people for such a City and said: *"Therefore your gates shall be open continually; they shall not be shut day nor night"* (Isaiah 60:11).

"And I John saw the holy city, the New Jerusalem coming down from God out of heaven" (Revelation 21:2), ... *"And the gates of it shall not be shut at all by day: for there shall be no night there"* (Revelation 21:25).

I point this out, because Melody said the gate where she was taken "opened inward," yet the gates of the New Jerusalem never close. The Bible helps us understand what was revealed to her. It shows us that Heaven is more than the New Jerusalem.

"In that day shall this song be sung in the land of Judah; We have a strong city; salvation will God appoint for walls and bulwarks. Open the gates, that the righteous nation which keeps the truth may enter in" (Isaiah 26:1-2).

In Christ, we are that nation:

"But you are a chosen generation, a royal priesthood, an holy nation..." (I Peter 2:9).

Needed: A Valid Passport
OUR CITIZENSHIP IS IN HEAVEN
(PHILIPPIANS 3:20)

Dollie and I minister in India. When we return to the U.S.A. we are required to have valid passports that prove we have citizenship in this country. We show our passports and pass freely through the gates. The Bible tells how Jesus purchased our heavenly citizenship with His own blood in the battle of the ages. Then He arose from the dead and entered the gates before us, as angels shouted His praises:

"Lift up your heads, O you gates!
And be lifted up, you everlasting doors!
And the King of glory shall come in.
Who is this King of glory? The LORD,
strong and mighty, The LORD mighty in battle.
Lift up your heads, O you gates!
Lift up, you everlasting doors! And the
King of glory shall come in. Who is this King of
glory? The LORD of hosts, He is the King of
glory!" (Psalm 24:7-9)

In Christ, we enter Heaven:

"This hope we have as an anchor of the soul, both sure and steadfast, and which enters the Presence behind the veil, where the forerunner has entered for us, even Jesus, having become High Priest forever after the order of Melchize-dek" (Hebrews 6:19-20).

"Blessed are those who do His commandments, that they may have the right to the tree of life, and may enter through the gates into the city" (Revelation 22:14-15).

In the merits of Jesus, in the innocence of a child, Melody stood before a gate. It was a massive gate that towered above the angels that guarded it.

Next:
God's Prophetic Voice In The Words Of A
Little Child

When our five-year-old daughter first told this story, Dollie and I began to make extensive notes. Later, a fellow-minister read these notes and wrote:

"There's no way this little girl could give so much profound Truth with her limited knowledge and language skills. It has a prophetic ring, a message from God. But if you print it as you have transcribed it, some people will not understand what God is saying. Some will think it's just another religious fable and will never read it. Others will try to make it say what their own imaginations concur.

Larry, the Lord has called you, and you're her dad. I suggest that you ask God to help bring insights of Scripture into this amazing story. Give readers the interpretation that He gives to you. They will understand your heart, and they will be grateful."

"A prophetic ring... a Message from God."

With words on the previous page in mind, we don't mean to be too "preachy." Yet, we feel that we must continue sharing our view of Melody's story. And she would have it no other way.

These thoughts are our own insights into her account. She certainly claimed no special gift of her own; yet friends who read what we had written down felt that God was speaking to us through her experience.

Over the years, we have found that to be so. The pages that follow are some deeper insights into what burns within our spirits, and what motivates us to serve Him.

"In this next part of Melody's
story, it is evident that God drew
her to us the first time. He lifted her
back to Himself. Then, He sent her
back to us to tell his message."

The Big Angels

God Makes a Big Statement to accent His Covenant.

What we discovered next is incredible! Little did this small, adopted child understand how God was weaving her out-of-body visitation into His pattern for our own lives. Nor could she have fathomed what the Lord would reveal to us as we searched the Bible for more light on her story. Only God knows the depth of our search, and we marvel at His response.

David declared, *"Deep calls unto deep at the noise of your waterspouts"* (Psalm 42:7).

A waterspout is a tornado at sea, pulling things to itself, lifting them up, and thrusting them out. In this next part of Melody's story, it is evident that God drew her to us the first time. He lifted her back to Himself. Then, He sent her back to us to tell His message!

In her short excerpt that follows, God concealed the Plan, the Mission, and the Message of our lives and ministry.

"It is the glory of God to conceal a thing: but the honor of kings is to search out a matter" (Proverbs 25:2).

As Melody continued...

She said, *"When I looked back, the angel that brought me to the gate was gone. In front of me, I saw a very large, shiny, pearl gate. There were two large angels, one on each side of the gate. Connected to the gate were walls on either side that stretched farther than I could see. Everything on the outside around me was still black; even over the top of the gate it was dark. The only things in color were the street, the gate, and the angels."*

"The two angels had long hair and their wings went above their heads and came down just below their feet. They were dressed in white and shiny clothing, and each one held a BIG sword. They did not talk. As big and as strong as they were, I still was not afraid."

Remember: An angel *"the size of a normal person"* had brought Melody to the gate, and suddenly had left. Now, she stands before this "massive" gate that she later described in an interview as *"over two stories high, and the two giant angels not quite as high."* In checking this, God was saying something BIG to us -- *SOMETHING REALLY BIG!*

Here, we see:

1. God's Big Salvation Plan.

2. God's Big World Mission.

3. God's Big Bible Message.

Let us look at the scene that Melody describes, and consider these points in the light of Scripture:

1. God's Big Salvation Plan.

Melody's Story: *"Connected to the gate, there were walls on either side that stretched farther than I could see."*

The Bible: These walls are the *"walls of salvation"* that enclose the inhabitants of this glorious place:

"But you shall call your walls Salvation, and your gates shall be called Praise. God shall be the Glory of His People. The sun shall no longer be your light by day, nor for brightness shall the moon give light to you; But the LORD will be to you an everlasting light, and your God shall be

your glory" (Isaiah 60:18-19).

"In that day this song will be sung in the land of Judah: We have a strong city; and God makes salvation its walls and ramparts" (Isaiah 26:1).

There is no salvation without a Savior. These walls of salvation stretch "further than we can see," and we must increase our vision to reach others for Jesus.

2. God's Big World Mission.

Melody's Story: *"Everything on the outside was dark. The only things in color were the street, the gate, and the angels."*

The Bible: *"Arise, shine, for your light has come, and the glory of the LORD rises upon you. See, darkness covers the earth and thick darkness is over the peoples, but the LORD rises upon you and his glory appears over you. Nations will come to your light..."* (Isaiah 60:1-3).

"But you are a chosen generation, a royal priesthood, an holy nation, a peculiar people, that you should shew forth the praises of him who hath called you out of darkness into his wonderful light" (1 Peter 2:9).

"After this I beheld and, lo, a great multitude which no man could number, of all nations,

kindred's, people, and tongues..." "And cried with a loud voice; saying Salvation belongs to our God, which sitteth upon the throne, and unto the Lamb" (Revelation 7:9-10).

3. God's Big Bible Message.

In the beginning, *"God said, „Let us make man in Our image... in the image of God He created him, male and female He created them"* (Genesis 1:26-28).

When Adam and Eve disobeyed God, and He drove them from the garden, we then read the first mention of angels: *"He placed cherubim at the east of the garden of Eden, and a flaming sword which turned every way, to guard the way to the tree of life"* (Genesis 3:24).

The Bible is focused on getting mankind back to God. As the descending seed of Adam, all people were separated from Him, and could not help themselves. The unfinished tower of Babel gave witness to their futile attempt, as *"the Lord scattered them from there over all the earth, and they stopped building the city. That is why it was called Babel... From there the LORD scattered them over the face of the whole earth"* (Genesis 11:8, 9).

God was not pleased with their humanistic

plan, but He still loved the people. He dispersed them into many nations, but in that same chapter, we see Him drawing Abram out of Ur (Genesis 11:26). God gave him the new name Abraham, meaning *"father of a multitude"* (Genesis 17:1; 15-19). The Lord told him, *"in your seed all the nations of the earth shall be blessed"* (Genesis 22:18; 26:4; 28:14).

The apostle Paul wrote:

"Now to Abraham and his Seed were the promises made. He does not say, 'seeds' as of many, but as of one, 'And to your Seed,' who is Christ... And if you are Christ's, then you are Abraham's seed, and heirs according to the promise" (Galatians 3:16-29). As we preach and teach the Message of Christ, we take the blessing of Abraham to the nations.

Next:

From the Cherubim in Eden to the Cherubim in Solomon's Temple, Some Big Angels confirm Melody's story.

Later, Abraham was set to offer his son Isaac on *Mount Moriah* in sacrifice. God halted him. A ram was offered instead, and Isaac was spared from death *"in a figure"* of Christ's resurrection (Genesis 22:2-13; Hebrews 11:19). Abraham called the place *"Jehovah-jireh,"* meaning *"in the Mount of the Lord it shall be seen."*

The next time that Moriah is mentioned, it is the location of Solomon's Temple.

"Then Solomon began to build the house of the Lord at Jerusalem in Mount Moriah" (2 Chronicles 3:1).

First, let us understand that Solomon's Temple was built for one reason, to hold the *Ark of the Covenant.*

The Ark was a chest-like container, carried upon the shoulders of the Levites. Inside the Ark were the tables of stone on which God had written His Covenant. Above the Ark was the mercy seat. It was one solid piece, like a lid, that covered the Ark, with two cherubim, one on each end. The cherubim looked down on the blood sprinkled there, shed to bring people back to God (Leviticus 16).

The tables of stone were crying out: *"Lord, people have broken Your law! Vengeance!*

Punishment!" But the blood was above, crying, *"Mercy! Mercy!"* Because of the blood, God heard the cry of mercy above the cry of the law, and He came to dwell with His people.

The mercy seat was God's seat. This was His portable throne among the people, as the pattern was made right for His Presence.

"Give ear, O Shepherd of Israel, You who lead Joseph like a flock; the One who dwells between the cherubim, shine forth" (Psalm 80:1; Isaiah 37:16).

Heaven Revealed

House Of The Big Angels

Total Wingspans: Thirty Feet!

One day, King David told Nathan the prophet, *"I dwell in a house of cedar, but the Ark of the Covenant of the Lord is under tent curtains"* (1 Chronicles 17:1). He had a heart to build a permanent house for the Ark.

This pleased God. That night He told Nathan, *"Go tell David that because he has a heart to make a house for the Ark, My mercy will never depart from his house."*

Fast forward 28 generations, from David to Christ (Matthew 1:17). Throughout His ministry, people were crying out, *"Jesus, Son of David, have mercy on us!"*

This pictures for us why God placed so many BIG things inside Solomon's Temple, to illustrate the coming glory of Christ.

The tabernacle of Moses had one laver that

was mirror-lined and filled with water; *the temple had ten lavers -- plus a giant sea that held 255,000 gallons!* (Exodus 30:38; 1 Kings 7:38-43; 1 Chronicles 4:5). And the number of animal sacrifices was a foreshadow of the priceless value of our redemption in Christ:

"King Solomon, and all the congregation of Israel who were assembled with him, were with him before the Ark, sacrificing sheep and oxen that could not be counted or numbered for multitude. Then the priests brought in the Ark of the Covenant of the Lord to its place, into the inner sanctuary of the temple, to the Most Holy Place, under the wings of the cherubim. For the cherubim spread their two wings over the place of the Ark, and the cherubim overshadowed the Ark..." (1 Kings 8:5-7).

"The wings of these cherubim spread themselves forth twenty cubits: and they stood on their feet, and their faces were inward" (2 Chronicles 3:13).

Her story said they towered toward the top of a gate that was maybe two stories high.

God Himself sized the Angels in Solomon's Temple:

"Total Wingspans: Thirty Feet"

How's that for a five-year-old child's story?

"THE WINGS OF THESE CHERUBIM SPREAD THEMSELVES FORTH TWENTY CUBITS"

(2 Chronicles 3:13).

A *cubit* was a biblical measurement, the average distance from the elbow to the tip of the fingers, measuring *one and one-half feet*. The total wingspan of the angels in Solomon's Temple was 20 cubits, or 30 feet. This puts them about the size that Melody saw in her visitation. But this is only the imagery or foreshadow of Heaven. It illustrates Christ-centered truths that are far more exceeding in glory.

Go back with me to the scene earlier, outside Eden's garden. The first human pair had lost God's favor, and were kept from their life-source by cherubim that guarded the gate.

Now, let us come forward to *The Day of Atonement* (Leviticus 16), where God has made provision for mankind to be at-one with Him through the blood of His sacrifice. There, watching over the Covenant, are two cherubim. They are there to serve God's interest, guarding the treasure of His heart, the holy oracles that bring mankind back to Himself. Just as surely as the cherubim kept man from Eden, that is how surely they guard the way back to the Father.

You see the depth of God's dedication to reach mankind, and you search the dedication of your own heart to make it so.

With Paul, you say,

"Preaching the Good News is not something I can boast about. I am compelled by God to do it. How terrible for me if I didn't do it!" (1 Corinthians 9:16) (NLT)

What is the essence of it all?

The Ark of the Covenant expressed *"the faithful God, which keeps covenant and shows mercy to them that love him and keep his commandments, even to a thousand generations"* (Deuteronomy 7:9).

One day Moses went to God, and *"he heard the voice of one speaking to him from off the mercy seat upon the ark of testimony from between the two cherubim"* (Numbers 7:89).

Today, we come *"to Jesus the Mediator of the*

New Covenant, and to the blood of sprinkling, that speaks better things than that of Abel" (Hebrews 12:24).

Abel's blood cried, *"Judgment!"* (Genesis 4:8-11), Christ's blood cries, *"Mercy!"*

We come to Him *"Whom God put forward... as a Mercy Seat and Propitiation by His blood"* (Romans 3:25) (Amp). And He meets us there.

The Bible says:

"He is the propitiation (Mercy Seat[1]) for our sins: and not for ours only, but also for the sins of the whole world" (1 John 2:2).

As revealed to us through Melody's visitation in Heaven...

We see God's *Plan* of Salvation;

We share God's *Mission* of World Evangelism;

We proclaim God's *Message* of Jesus.

" I HAD JUST THOUGHT IT, AND HE SPOKE IT OUT LOUD,

'MELODY, THERE ARE NO STICKERS IN HEAVEN.'"

[1]See Romans 3:25 in the Amplified Bible, and Vine's Expository Dictionary of New Testament Words

Heaven Revealed

"There Are No Stickers In Heaven"

When she came back to us, Melody said she had seen Jesus while she was in Heaven. We had many questions, as most people would. When asked, Melody always answered, *"He had long hair and dark eyes. He also had a beard." She recalls that Jesus appeared to be a normal size man, and His skin was like hers.*

What does that mean? She had been in the sun a lot that summer, and she gets a dark tan quickly. So to her, He was not of light skin, but He had a tanned complexion like hers. "He wore a white robe with a gold belt," she said.

The New Testament has recorded many instances where people saw Jesus in His resurrected body. In one chapter alone, the apostle Paul mentions over 500 people who saw Him at once (1 Corinthians 15:6). Many writers have referred to His resurrection as "the most attested fact in history."

It appears that the resurrected Jesus reveals Himself as He pleases. Mary thought Him *"the gardener"* (John 20:15). Two on Emmaus Road saw Him in *"another form"* Mark 26:12. But the martyr Stephen said, *"Behold, I see the heavens opened, and the Son of man standing on the right hand of God"* (Acts 7:56).

John said that Jesus wore *"a golden girdle..."* and *"His feet were like fine brass, as if... burned in a furnace"* (Revelation 1:13-16). Young Melody said He wore a gold belt and His skin had a dark tan color (like bronze).

The child was right-on with the Bible!

One of the highlights of this remarkable story is when Melody and Jesus were walking together. She was so impressed with His personable compassion toward her; He knew even her thoughts, before she could speak them. As she told about this, it was obvious that this particular insight would minister to many people.

Melody said they were walking in a grassy area, and she was in her bare feet. In Tyler, Texas, she had often feared walking on "sand burrs"-- a small, yet painful "sticker" that she would step on. As they walked together in

Heaven, she thought, *"I hope I don't get stickers in my feet."* Even as she thought it, having yet said nothing, Jesus said, *"Melody, there are no stickers in Heaven!"*

Years later at the age of sixteen she said not all communication was verbal but she would think a thought and the answer would just come from Jesus into her mind.

The scriptures say there are no stickers in Heaven. When Adam and Eve disobeyed Him, the Lord said: *"cursed is the ground for your sake; in sorrow you shall eat of it all the days of your life. Thorns also and thistles shall it bring forth..."* (Genesis 3:17-18).

We know that these thorns and thistles are part of earth's curse. The curse has no part of Heaven, for *"there shall be no more curse: but the throne of God and of the Lamb shall be in it"* (Revelation 22:3).

If you have lived in an area that has sand burrs, you have perhaps heard the cry of children, as these thorny stickers pierce their feet. You will understand how this little girl was so impressed that Jesus assured her:

"Melody, there are no stickers in Heaven."

That's how the Bible describes Jesus:

"We do not have a High Priest who cannot be touched with the feeling of infirmities, but was in all points tempted as we are, yet without sin. Let us therefore come boldly to the throne of grace, that we may obtain mercy and find grace to help in time of need" (Hebrews 4:15-16).

The Personable Jesus; He is Touched with Your Hurts.

Jesus knows very much what it's like to have pierced feet. In a prophecy of His crucifixion, David wrote: *"The assembly of the wicked have enclosed me: they pierced my hands and my feet"* (Psalm 22:16).

There are no evil stickers in Heaven, like those at His crucifixion. There are no *nails*, or *spears*, or *thorns*, or *the piercing words* of His accusers. He overcame them all, and reigns forever as our *Personal Savior* and *Personable Mediator*.

The apostle John gave an eyewitness account of this piercing: *"One of the soldiers with a spear pierced his side, and forthwith came there out blood and water. And he that saw it bare record, and his record is true: and he knows what he says is true, that you might believe. For these things were done, that the scripture should be fulfilled, A bone of him shall not be broken, and again another scripture says, They shall look on him whom they pierced"* (John 19:34-37).

An Old Testament prophecy declared:

"And one shall say unto him, what are these wounds in your hands? Then he shall answer, those with which I was wounded in the house of my friends" (Zechariah 13:6).

In what follows, Dollie finds release from thoughts that had stuck in her mind since childhood. It had to do with something that happened while Melody was in Heaven, something that neither Dollie nor I had ever spoken of, but this child spoke things that only Heaven could have revealed.

A background...

From the beginning, we had an affinity with Melody. Dollie also had been adopted. The marriage of her birth parents lasted but a short time. When she was just a baby, her mother moved with her into the home of an aunt, Betty Lee Cox.

In the pressures of life, the young mother became persuaded that this aunt should have complete charge of Dollie. And so it was that

Betty Cox eventually arranged for Dollie to become her adopted daughter.

So, an unmarried, great aunt, reared Dollie. It was a difficult lifestyle. Ms. Cox was quite eccentric, and was not easy to live with, to say the least. This was never a normal, loving, mother-daughter relationship. Dollie could never remember Ms. Cox telling her that she was loved. These doubts and questions continued to plague her even into our marriage. *But this was changed when our own child told what happened in Heaven.*

Before this part of the story, Melody saw a beautiful body of water, and other things that were so personal to her. We talk about them later. But next, she introduces us to the setting for Dollie's experience.

"After this," she said, *"I remember being in the middle of houses and trees. The houses were small and there were trees in between them."* She did not know how to describe what these houses were made of.

Dollie asked if they were painted, and Melody said, *"They were not like houses I've seen."* They were not wood or brick and she didn't know how to describe them. Then, finally she said, *"They were like stones in rings."* We interpreted that to mean either precious or semi-precious stones. We could think of nothing in the Bible that described the material of such houses. Yet, it seemed to us God would make them from precious stones like *"the foundation of the wall"* of the New Jerusalem, which is made of 12 manners of precious stones (Revelation 21:19, 20).

Melody began to tell her mother the colors of these houses; some were outside colors and some were inside colors. Some had one floor and some also had a second floor. Dollie began to make a diagram of little square boxes for the houses and abbreviated the color of each house in the boxes as Melody told her.

The diagram was very detailed. One house was round and like glass at the end of the first row of houses. At the end of the second row of houses was a triangle-shaped house that was silver, studded with diamonds. At the end of the third row of houses was a green house with a gate leading to a pool. One house was red and orange with a big "C" on the door. Between the houses was an area for the children to play. One area was where older children played and one area was for smaller children. She described one house as being like *"brown diamonds."* Later we discovered, there are such things as brown diamonds!

I arrived home about three or four hours later, after Melody had told her mother about these houses. Dollie told me this story and handed me the descriptive diagram. I was thinking, *I don't know about this. It sounds too detailed to me. Sounds like someone is fantasizing or making stuff up.*

I knew that Melody had never been a child to fantasize or to make up stories. So, I laid the paper with the diagram that Dollie had drawn down in front of Melody. I began to ask her the colors of the different houses in each row. I pointed to each house and asked her the color. I went through every house on the diagram, and she told me exactly the same colors that she had told Dollie three to four hours earlier.

Remember, she had just turned five about four weeks prior to this. She had not learned to read yet. She could not read the names Dollie had written anyway, for each name was abbreviated. To me, it was still so fresh in her mind that she could instantly tell me all she had told Dollie earlier. And even though I didn't understand it, this super-cautious daddy knew he had to check it out.

As to this little child going to Heaven and still being in her five-year-old body, I read scriptures that support this: *"To be absent from the body, is to be present with the Lord"* (2 Corinthians 5:8). This fact is not limited by the age or size of the body. David knew his departed baby was there, and said, *"I shall go to him"* (2 Samuel 12:24). As to Melody inter-acting with other children in Heaven, the Bible says that *we will know as we are known* (I Corinthians 13:12). As to the houses that Dollie diagrammed, there could be no better insight than the old, respected commentary of Matthew Henry (next page). He says that in Heaven we flow together, yet dwell "a part" -- in something like *"heavenly apartments."*

**MATTHEW HENRY COMMENTARY ON HEAVEN --
John 14:1-3.**

There are mansions there; that is: First, Distinct dwellings, an apartment for each. Perhaps this is an allusion to the priests' chambers that were about the temple. In Heaven, there are accommodations for particular saints; though all shall be swallowed up in God, yet our individuality shall not be lost there; every Israelite had his lot in Canaan, and every elder a seat (Revelation 4:4). Secondly, durable dwellings: Monai, from mneio, maneo, abiding places.

The house itself is lasting; our estate in it is not for a term of years, but perpetuity. Here we are as in an inn; in Heaven we shall gain a settlement...

This story continues on page 96, telling how Melody saw Dollies' mother in Heaven. A sketch of the houses she described to Dollie is printed on page 99.

Heaven Revealed

Heaven Revealed

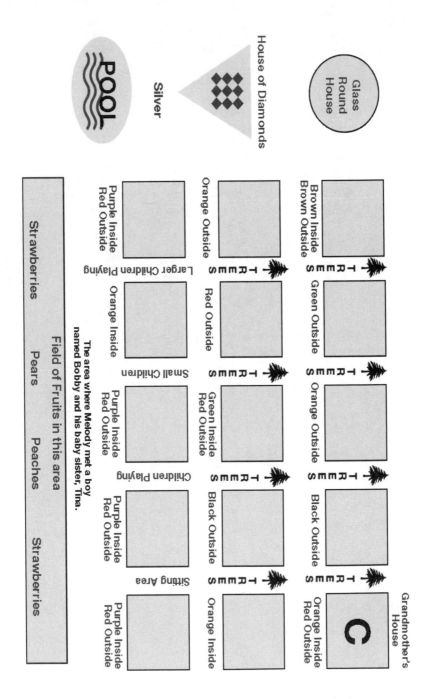

When I talk about this part of her story in our meetings, I say, "You will note the big "C"on the house in the top corner. This is where Melody met her grandmother, Ms. Cox (Dollie's mother), who died when Melody was only nine months old."

I have explained this drawing in detail already on previous pages. You may want to use it as a cross-reference to what you have already read. This gives some idea of what God has revealed to us personally. To try and explain every detail would certainly require much more than the allotted pages.

Heaven Revealed

"I Saw Your Mother."

At one point Dollie asked Melody if she had seen anyone in Heaven that she or we knew. To her absolute astonishment, Melody replied, *"Yes, I saw your mother who died."*

It was an answer like, *"Yes, I've wanted to say something about this. But we've been talking about Jesus, and Heaven's big gates, and gold street, and angels, and..."* Yes, there was plenty she had to tell about Dollie's mother; simple, yet profound things. In one of her interviews, she begins to tell how it happened...

"Suddenly, I was standing in front of this red house. The door had a big 'C' on the front of it. I don't recall the door ever opening, but I found myself standing inside looking around. I was in the living room and there were rooms to my left, the kitchen was in front of me, and there was a room with a table to my right. I could tell that this house had plenty of places to live in, but it looked like whoever lived here

stayed mostly in the living room and kitchen. I could see someone standing in the kitchen at the counter making something. Instantly, I knew -- it was like a deep-inside knowing -- that this was the mother of my mother, and I was standing in her house. The funny thing is I don't remember to this day ever seeing this lady's face. I saw her standing in the kitchen, and remember seeing her body and her arms, and when she brought what she had been making, a bowl of..."

Melody did not know her grandmother on earth, as she was only nine months old when Ms. Cox died. We did not happen to have a picture of her in our home where Melody lived, so she could not have even recognized her from a photograph.

She described Ms. Cox's house in Heaven as being red outside and orange inside. These, would you believe, were her favorite colors.

Melody went on to describe other things about her house, telling us it was a big house, but it seemed Ms. Cox lived mainly in one large room. This was typical of the way this eccentric lady did live on earth. She would bring all the furnishings together into one main room, even though she had many rooms. At times, she even slept in a recliner in that same room.

And the bowl that Ms. Cox had prepared, the one Melody saw her bring from the kitchen? It was a bowl of *fruit salad*. Melody said she was served this delicious meal. And we knew it was one of Ms. Cox's favorite foods.

It's obvious what the big "C" on her door meant. It's the initial of her last name.

It was as though this child had read some family diary from the past, yet we knew she could not read. It became apparent to us that God revealed these things. And they certainly prepared Dollie to receive what He would reveal next.

Dollie asked Melody what Ms. Cox had said to her. Melody replied, "We talked a long time, but I can't remember anything she said, except...

And this is the key to this entire story.

If nothing else, this testifies to the veracity of a five-year-old's miracle visit to Heaven.

Because what she was about to say, she could in no way have known its significance to Dollie. Melody replied, *"I can't remember anything she said, except 'tell your mother that I love her!'"*

Dollie could never remember hearing those

words from Ms. Cox. Never in that earthly home had she heard these words. But out of Melody's drowning experience and visit to Heaven, God sent a message to Dollie from her mother's heavenly home!

Now, Dollie knew that she was loved even though she had never heard those words from her mother's lips while she was on earth!

It is interesting that one of our greatest battles is in the field of our mind, and Jesus received one of His wounds when the thorns pierced His brow. The Bible records how this took place...

"Then Pilate took Jesus, and scourged him. And the soldiers platted a crown of thorns, and put it on his head, and they put on him a purple robe, And said, Hail, King of the Jews! and they smote him with their hands. Pilate therefore went forth again, and said to them, Behold, I bring him forth to you, that you may know that I find no fault in him" (John 19:1-4).

What a terrible injustice! Pilate actually punished Jesus, then he declared Him to be innocent, saying, *"I find no fault in Him!"* Why? Because Pilate had no power over what was happening (John 19:11). This was by God's design, the Innocent (Jesus) suffering for the guilty (all mankind).

That means the Innocent Jesus took our *wounds* upon *Himself.* And when we believe this and come to Him, the justice of God will not permit Him to leave upon us what He has already put upon Jesus.

In the original language of the New Testament, some words for *"wound"* are *"trauma,* or *traumaizo,* or *traumatizoo."*[1] Because of Jesus, it is not the Will of God for any believer to be traumatized.

This applies to the old and the young.

The Lord ministered to Dollie through Melody's visitation in Heaven.

One of the first things that Melody saw when she entered the gate was what she called *"a pond"* -- *a body of water.* This is so like the *"Personable Jesus"* that we mentioned earlier. He freed her from the fear of what took her life.

Her last view of earth was threatening water. Her first view of Heaven is refreshing water.

As she recalls it: *"When I entered, I was standing in an area that had green grass and flowers, and it was so pretty. I remember there*

[1]See Strongs #5134; 5135; Thayer's Greek Lexicon; and
Vine's Expository Dictionary of New Testament Words.

were kids everywhere, playing and running around. There was even this pond that had the clearest water I'd ever seen. It was like glass. I remember thinking how clear it was. The pool at papaw's (Pastor Sluder's) house would get leaves and things in it, but I did not see anything like that in this pond. The kids were playing in the pond, and when they'd go into the water they would be wet but when they would come out they were dry!

The area around the pond had flowers and trees and was so bright and pretty. There were fruit trees and bushes, and everybody was eating whatever their favorite fruit was but sharing with one another." (The children were even playing with their pets; see 'animals in Heaven' on page 109.)

At this point, the analogies are over. There's no need to further clarify the *"water that's like glass"* and the rejoicing of little children. The pages of God's Book reveal those things, and those who love Truth will do their own search. Now, the scenes that Melody describes are just a backdrop to what the Lord is saying through her story.

Remember at the beginning, back at the

swimming pool in Tyler, Texas? We read it again from Chapter Four...

"She had been playing at the pool with the Sluders' oldest daughter, Pat, who was ready to leave. Pat fastened her float to the buoy rope. Then: the rope was hooked to the side of the pool. Melody had taken the buoy rope no longer in use, and she tied it around her own little plastic ring. When Melody returned, her buoy rope had come loose... She decided to walk out and get it..."

Melody was there alone so she devised a way to "swim" in shallow water. She wanted to share her idea with us, but failed to get our attention. She returned to the pool. The buoy rope was loose, out in the middle of the pool. She was unable to swim in deep water. There was no one to help.

That's how our story began, with this little girl in water over her head, her body floating face-down.

Moments later, her spirit is in Heaven. The *trauma* of her drowning is gone. She no longer has the fear of being isolated from others. She is with children like herself, no longer alone, as she had been back at the swimming pool. In the

Presence of Jesus, there is joy and together-ness in this Wonderful Place. And she's getting on with *real Life.*

Jesus designed it that way. Whether out of the body in Heaven, or in the body on earth, our real purpose is to share His Life.

This life-principle kept working in little Melody, even as she was in Heaven.

For while there, she was already looking beyond her own *trauma* to the hurts of people on earth...

Later, Melody shared this in one of her interviews:

"At some point while I was in this area, I started talking to a little boy whose name was Bobby. He had a little baby sister named Tina. To this day, I don't really remember what they looked like, or what we did. But I remember holding baby Tina."

"After coming back, I named all my baby dolls Tina. Mom said that while I was first telling her this story, I came really close to saying what had happened to them, to cause them to end up in Heaven together. But she said when I got close to telling it, I just got quiet, and stopped

talking. She was going to try and find the family, and let them know I'd seen their children, but I didn't give her enough information."

Melody has expressed many times how she regrets that she could not say more about these two children. She felt that maybe the parents who lost these children would be helped by her story. I think it is because God chooses to conceal some things, to be revealed in His timing. It could be that some mom or dad who lost a boy named Bobby and a little baby girl named Tina will read this, and will rejoice to know they can see them again in Heaven.

I do know that since that day, Melody has moved on beyond what could have been life-long *trauma*. Her heart is to reach people who are hurting. As she ministers, she always rejoices to hear about others who have been through a similar experience.

She receives feedback from others...

"During the whole time I had been in Heaven, behind everything I saw and all places I went, in the distance there was a greenish, cloudy haze. It sort of kept me from seeing anything beyond where I was.

Once I spoke to a minister who had a similar

experience as mine. As we talked, the room *filled with a Presence so thick I could have cut it with a knife. I had never before had that happen when I told the story. Maybe it was because this minister had such strong agreement with what I was saying, for he knew these things by experience. When I mentioned to him about the greenish haze, something I didn't usually tell other people, he asked if I knew what that was. I told him I didn't. He said, 'That is the Cloud of the Presence of God that surrounds the Throne.' Amazing!"*

"...and there was a rainbow round about the throne, in sight like unto an emerald" (Revelation 4:3).

Since the emerald is green in color, this could well be the "greenish" haze that Melody saw in Heaven. She continued...

"Once at a church in Trenton, Kentucky, there was a little boy in the audience who had lost an arm in a farming accident. He was only about ten years old, I think. I didn't know his story until after I was finished speaking. His mother told me that when he had his accident, he had died on the table. They were able to bring him back, and for a long time he never told what

happened to him. I think that even up until that night, he had not told them many details at all. But while I was speaking, he was in the sound room next to the pastor, listening. The pastor said that throughout my message, the boy kept telling him, 'I saw that! I saw that too!' This confirmed to the boy that his own out-of-body experience was very real. It actually helped to confirm to me that my story was real."

I think how much we treasured this special child that God brought into our lives, and how her tragic drowning absolutely crushed our hearts. Then, I am reminded that the prophet said Christ would *"bind up the broken hearted"* (Isaiah 61:2; Luke 4:18).

That is what happened, especially in those first days, as God's people rallied around us.

The Lord brought them to us. They began to *"bind up our wounds"* like the good Samaritan that Jesus told about in Luke's Gospel (10:34).

But there came a time when God spoke more of that scripture: *"I must set at liberty them that are bruised"* (Luke 4:18). And His people began to help us *loose the bindings from our wounds* and get on with life.

O, how we appreciate the people of God!

Heaven Revealed

"He comforts us in all our troubles so that we can comfort others. When others are troubled, we will be able to give them the same comfort God has given us" (2 Corinthians 1:4) (NLT).

We thank God that He sent Melody back to us, and through His compassionate people, He helped us look beyond our trauma...

- to find a need and fill it;
- to find a hurt and heal it.

Just think what little of
Heaven is revealed in a
child's few earth-minutes
with Jesus! Then think: In the
endless eternity, His endless
revelations will relate to each
of us personally!

"Do You Want To Stay Or Go Back?"

God gave her a choice between Life and Life!

Earlier, we mentioned Melody's special walk with Jesus, where He assured her *"There are no stickers in Heaven."* She says, "At other times, *it was not so much walking, but just thinking about being at a place, and you were suddenly there."*

The apostle John heard a voice say, *"Come up here, and I will show you things which must take place after this."* He said, *"Immediately I was in the Spirit; and behold, a throne set in heaven..."* (Revelation 4:1-2). Being *"in the Spirit"* is the key to our communication and walk with God.

The Bible says: *"The Spirit Himself bears witness with our spirits that we are the children of God"* (Romans 8:16). You *"receive the adoption of sons. And because you are sons,*

God has sent forth the Spirit of his Son into your hearts, crying, Abba, Father" (Galatians 4:5-6).

This helps you see the deep relationship that we had with our own "adopted daughter." On earth, Melody had already grown to love us and to obediently respond to our voices. Our relationship with her was even surer. We had searched specifically for her and had chosen her as our own. We loved her dearly, and we cared very much about her deepest desires, even her tastes for food.

This is a picture of every believer's adoption in God. It is not just our relationship with Him, but, *it is His relationship with us, to which the Spirit gives witness!* That is why I was so impressed with what happened to Melody next while she was in Heaven -- just before Jesus released her and sent her back to us. Let me explain.

With all our hearts, Dollie and I chose to serve Him, yet He said, *"I no longer call you servants, for a servant does not know what his master is doing; but I have called you friends..."* (John 15:15). Although I do not fully understand what happened next, I am humbled to think that Jesus did it to send us a message that He is our Friend.

It is like some good thing you would do for a daughter of your own friends, before you send her back -- a fresh memory of your friendship.

Dollie and I knew that Melody had a keen taste for strawberries. These are her favorite fruit. Melody said she was in a field in Heaven, and she sensed a strong Presence. She realized that Jesus was behind her, even before she turned. He took her by the hand and led her into a field of strawberries. He gave her a taste of these, just before He sent her back to us.

It was like He was saying to us, *"I know how much you care for her, even to her favorite food. How much more do I care for her in Heaven."* What a Friend we have in Jesus!

When little Melody told her mother about this after she returned from Heaven, she said, *"They were the bestest strawberries I ever ate!"*

The Bible says that God's people will be eating in Heaven (See page 112). What is the food of Heaven like, and how does it taste? We will know Heaven's full answer when we get there. The Bible gives a partial-answer in the food that God once sent down to His people. It's first name was "what is it." *"They said to each other, "What is it?" For they did not know what it was"* (Exodus 16:15). Then they called it *"Manna."* To some *"it tasted like wafers made with honey"* (v. 31). To others, *"it was as the taste of fresh oil"* (Numbers 11:8). And the psalmist said that God *"rained down manna upon them to eat, and had given them of the corn of heaven. Man did eat angels' food"* (Psalm 78:24-25).

Just think what little of Heaven is revealed in a child's few earth-minutes with Jesus! Then think: In the endless eternity, His endless revelations will relate to each of us personally!

Finally, Jesus released Melody back to us.

"After this, Jesus walked me over to the edge of Heaven. When I say edge, I mean it was like standing on the edge of a building, looking down to see what was going on below. I could still see those around my body at the pool. I could see my Papaw Sluder, trying to bring my body back to life. Jesus asked me, Do you want to stay here, or do you want to go back and see your mom and dad? I told Jesus that I wanted to think about it for a minute. I thought about it, but finally I told Him that I wanted to go back and see my mom and dad. Then He said, 'Ok. You can go back to them, and you can come back

here later.' At that point, I believe, is when my eye flickered, and I came back to life."

Melody always emphasizes that Jesus said, "you can come back later." To her, this meant that Jesus gave her a choice of Life in Heaven with Him right then, or *"you can return if you live My Life on earth."*

In the next and final chapter Melody shares her thoughts with you.

Heaven Revealed

One Final Thought

When Dad asked me to write the last chapter of this book, I had to agree that it seems like the most fitting way to end this story. I find that to hear from the person who actually lived the story adds a bit of personal intimacy and makes it even more real to whoever is reading the book. It's like watching a "true story" movie and seeing the person's face while the credits arc rolling. There comes this connection in your mind and heart to know that someone really did experience the story you just watched. And at times, you actually walk away from the movie inspired and, maybe, will even pass on the story to someone else who needs to hear a word of encouragement or hope. Although I can't show you my face, I can at least write to you as the one who really lived this experience. Perhaps it will help to bring an even stronger confirmation that the details are real and true.

There are a few things that I wish I could sit down and tell you in person…just you and me, at a table talking about the reality of Heaven. I'd love to see your eyes as you hear the details of the things I saw or hear your questions of what you've always wondered about your future home. Of course, there's always the one that most people can't wait to ask, "What did Jesus look like?" We've tried really hard to give you descriptions that will answer your questions, but I know that reading this book has probably stirred you beyond just description and details. I'm sure somewhere in your soul, you're asking about your own relationships with Christ. What would happen if you drowned or some other situation brought you to a place where you'd have to face eternity? Would you see the same thing I did? Would you see Jesus?

One of the most important things to me, when I speak to people about this experience, is the very last thing that Jesus said, "You can go back and you can come back later." The impact of that statement didn't hit me until I was much older. In those few short words lies the very essence of the grace and mercy of God. See, I wasn't given a free pass just because I'd seen Heaven once. There was no guarantee given that

I'd be back the next time around. Jesus laid out a choice for me. Can is a choice word. It takes you and me making a conscious effort to decide to choose eternal life. Jesus was saying to me, "Melody, just because you are a preacher's kid, and just because the future I have for you may hold years of ministry and telling other people about my salvation, it is still up to you to choose Me." At some point you are going to have to decide for yourself that you want to live for me, even when life entices you or leads you in other directions. Will you come back? It's up to you. What a heavy statement. What a challenge in my adulthood.

What about your life? Do you find yourself wondering after all of the years that you've lived, have you really chosen Jesus? Yes, you may have prayed as a young person at a youth camp or beside your bed one night, but possibly, as you've gotten older, that prayer seems like a very distant memory. Or you may think that since you did pray at a young age, it has lasted you through all the things you know haven't been right in your life, and maybe you've lived as though you've never needed to make an adult choice to serve God.

I don't know where you are spiritually; only you and God know that. But before you close this book, may I remind you of a few things? You're going to have to answer that question in your heart when you finish this, so I want to give you a few things to consider before you do.

First of all, I want to remind you that I'm nothing special. I don't know why God chose me to have this experience. Honestly, I'm not sure it would have been my first choice knowing how hard it would be on my family to live through those first few minutes of fear. Often times, I truly believe it was for my mother's sake and for the sake of those who hear this story. I was just a pawn in a greater plan. But as I think about some of the key points, I realize how much Jesus was really trying to say to all of us.

I recently heard a minister suggest why God used pearl to build the gates. I'm sure many of you know how a pearl is made. An oyster is created with a very sensitive inside tissue. Anytime a tiny speck of dirt is able to penetrate the outer shell and make its way into that tissue, the oyster immediately starts to cover the dirt with a substance to protect itself from the irritation that it would receive if that dirt was left alone. It coats it over and over again until that thing that had once been a wound, a source of pain for the oyster, now becomes a precious and valuable creation. Women, who adore pearls, wear around their necks a strand of wounds that have been healed.

Maybe God wanted to remind you as you consider the entrance to heaven that the wounds you live here on earth, the things that have damaged your mind, soul and spirit, will one day in Heaven be forever passed through. If you allow Jesus to coat over those wounds with His healing mercy, you will find that the situation that was once meant to destroy you is now a valuable reminder of God's personal attention to your life. When you get to Heaven, the first thing He will do for you is allow you to pass into eternity between gates of pearl into a place where all wounds are gone, never again to be remembered by you.

Secondly, please consider the number of details in the story that were so personal and intimate. Did you recognize how much He loves you? Enough to know your favorite color, your habits, likes and dislikes, your personality, even what you like to eat! He's not so far away that He doesn't know the least things about you. All those times you've wondered where God was and whether he cared. Look at the proof in this story! He knew my favorite food; He knew my thoughts, my fears and my worries. He knows you too. He knows your struggles, what you worry about, and what your fears are. He's not so distant that He can't see what you like and don't like. He knows what makes you smile, like a lover who is studying you to know how to please you, with flowers or your favorite book. God knows you inside and out. For some people that is a frightening thought. To be so exposed to someone and to trust them completely has, in the past, backfired and hurt them deeply. But if I could encourage you to open up to Jesus, a little at a time, and to let Him prove to you that you can trust Him, I assure you He will not fail.

I said earlier that I have often felt that this experience was for my mother. I want you to understand what I mean by that. As you read, mom grew up without ever knowing she was loved. She lived 30 plus years with a wound in her heart that she probably thought she'd just have to bear the rest of her life. No person can heal something like that in another's life. That's definitely a God-sized miracle. I wonder though, why He didn't just do it at an altar at a church somewhere. He could have met her in a personal time of devotion and shown her some scripture that would be the cure for all her pain. Why in the world would He allow a tragedy to be used to bring healing? I mean, at the moment she found me in the pool, I can't imagine she was thinking, "This is for my good. This is going to be the moment the pain of my past is going to be made well." She didn't know that the end of the story would turn out well. All she saw was what had the potential to be the most devastating day of her life.

Honestly, I don't know why He chose to do things the way He did. I don't understand His ways any more than you do. All I know is that through what seemed like the most tragic moment of her life, He was about to bring a deep, deep healing. If it is possible for you to grasp, God does use tragedy to bring healing. I want to be cautious about saying that God had it designed that I would drown, because I believe in the power of the consequences of human choice, but I do know that He was going to be sure my mother knew that He was ready and able to use whatever came her way to bind up her broken spirit. He wanted to let her know that He was aware that she had carried this pain long enough, and He was ready to take that pain away from her. I tend to think He didn't allow me to drown to prove a point; He used the consequence of my choice to show up and perform a miracle for my family instead! Not only to bring me back to life, but to heal my mom as well.

Why do I say this? Because maybe for you there has been a choice made that brought great tragedy into your life, maybe something you have done or someone else did to you. Humans definitely have been known to be the greatest pain givers there are. But be reminded that through the pain, God will come in and perform a miracle for you, too. It might not be raising someone from the dead or anything like that, but if you look and consider and ask Him where the miracle is, I believe you will find the answer in time. See, Mom had to take the initiative

and ask me, "Did anything happen when you drowned?" If she had not asked, she would never have found the words that were meant just for her.

You might have to do the same thing. Ask yourself why a tragedy has happened, or maybe ask the tragedy itself, "Why have you come? What is your purpose?" That's hard to do; trust me, I know. I recently had to ask the same thing. But after I looked it square in the face, I realized the answer was there. I walked through it and came out even stronger. God's hand was definitely in the process.

I don't know where you are in your life right now, but the time has come for you to consider the truths in this book. There is an eternity for you. Where that eternity is spent depends on what you do with the statement, "you can come back...." What will be your choice? If you weigh things out in your mind, it seems to me the choice is clear. Choose Jesus, the one who loves you more than you will ever understand. Choose the One who is willing to walk you through painful moments to help you find your healing. He is the one who is so in tune with you that He used the near death of a child and the momentary heartache of a family to reach out and let you know that He loves you.

If you've never made the decision, now is as good a time as any. Or if you've walked away from the relationship you once had with Jesus and are realizing that you must come back, this time is for you too.

"Jesus, my friend has been reading this book and has been contemplating their own eternity

with you. You see where they are, and you are ready to bring them close to your heart. You said yourself; you are close to the brokenhearted and you will bind up their wounds. You are the one who will walk with them through this life, and when it comes time for them to die, you will be waiting on the other side. Jesus, would you remind them that you died on the cross for their sins? That you are not angry with them or hold their sins against them? Wherever they are right now, close the deal with their souls. As they choose to live for you, let them know, beyond a shadow of a doubt, that you will not let go of them. Ever! Even when the tragedies come, you will be there.

Thank you for being in their room tonight and for rescuing their souls from an eternity without you. I look forward to seeing them someday, whether on this side of Heaven or the other."

I hope that you have decided today to choose life. I will be praying for you. Don't give up. The prize is worth it. Heaven is definitely real.

— Melody

ADDENDUM

Some researched Facts
Revealed in the Scriptures.

Will we have Personal Identity in Heaven?

In His resurrected body, Jesus was known on earth by His disciples for forty days, and "this same Jesus" will come again from Heaven (Acts 1:1-11). Moses and Elijah were still identifiable when they appeared with Jesus on a mount (Matthew 17:2,3). Lazarus still kept his identity (Luke 16). Our names are "written in Heaven" (Luke 10:20), in the Book of Life (Philippians 4:3), and names signify personal identity.

Will there be Eating in Heaven?

At the Last Supper, Jesus said his disciples would again "eat and drink with Him in the Kingdom" (Luke 22:16,30). And there will be "the marriage supper of the Lamb" (Revelation 19:9). Jesus gives an open invitation: *"I say to you that many will come from the east and the west, and will take their places at the feast with Abraham, Isaac and Jacob in the kingdom of heaven"* (Matthew 8:11) (NIV). We will cat of the tree of life (2:7) and hidden manna (2:17). However we describe the food, it will be heavenly!

Will there be Animals in Heaven?

The Bible pictures Jesus in Heaven, on a white horse (Revelation 6:2; 19:11). Under His earthly reign, there is no curse (Romans 8:19-33; Isaiah 55:13; 41:18, 19). Without the curse, wild animals are tame (Isaiah 11:6-9; 65:25; Ezekiel 34:25-28; Hosea 2:18). There will be no curse in Heaven (Revelation 22:3), so animals qualify to be there.

Heaven Revealed

Will there be Little Children in Heaven?

The scriptures say, "to be absent from the body is to be present with the Lord" (2 Corinthians 5:8). The Bible does not limit this to age or size. David knew his departed baby was there, and said, "I shall go to him" (2 Samuel 12:24). Under the earthly reign of Christ for 1,000 years -- a prelude to eternity in Heaven -- "a little child shall lead them" (Isaiah 11:6).

Bibliography

The Bible: Amplified Bible, © 1987 by The Zondervan Corporation and Lockman Foundation, Grand Rapids, Michigan.

King James Version, (1611); New King James Version;

American Standard Version; New Living Translation;

Vine's Expository Dictionary of New Testament Words;

Jamieson, Fausset & Brown Commentary;

Matthew Henry Commentary; Thayer's Greek Lexicon.

All Referenced from: Electronic Database,

Copyright © 2000, 2003 by Biblesoft, Inc.

Used in brief portions under the Right of Fair Use.

Reaching India

Through the various outreaches of Lighthouse Ministries, multitudes are seeing *Heaven Revealed* in the nation of India.

Some of the various arms of ministry are listed on the next page. To identify with what God is doing, to receive more information, or to arrange a meeting on the home front, you may contact Larry and Dollie at their address in this book.

The Meade Family Today:
Larry, Dollie and Melody, in the native dress of India.

Crusades:
From the beginning, this evangelistic thrust has taken the Gospel into remote regions where the voice of God is dim.

Church Planting:
Lighthouse Ministries continues to follow up the crusades in the building of national churches, and to help train pastors to shepherd God's people.

Supporting Pastors:
Through mentoring pastors, supplying motor scooters, motorcycles, etc., the Meades' extend their influence through the lives of others.

Women Conferences:
In team outreaches to women, the Lord heals and delivers many from bondages and baptizes believers in the Holy Spirit as the Word is ministered. Women who would want to go on one of these teams to the overseas field should contact Dollie.

Village Schools:
Schools are set up in villages where children otherwise would not receive an education. The first school already has 400 students, and the second over 225. Land has been purchased and the first phase of the school has been built and the second phase in progress.

Child Sponsorship:
Melody coordinates this sponsorship program that provides assistance to poor families so their children can have an education. This is a way that someone can "adopt" a child in India, and help them develop their hidden potential.

Heaven Revealed

The story inside is available in quantities to churches, ministries, or other groups. For more information, contact the address below. All proceeds are used in the work of God.

**Larry Meade
Lighthouse Ministries**

P.O. Box 754
Bardstown, KY 40004
U.S.A.
www.meadelighthouseministries.org

Heaven Revealed

Heaven Revealed

Heaven Revealed